# BRITAIN IN PICTURES
## THE BRITISH PEOPLE IN PICTURES

---

# THE PORT OF LONDON

GENERAL EDITOR
W. J. TURNER

The Editor is most grateful to all those who have
so kindly helped in the selection of illustrations
especially to officials of the various public
Museums Libraries and Galleries and
to all others who have generously
allowed pictures and MSS
to be reproduced

# THE
# PORT OF LONDON

## JOHN HERBERT

*WITH*
*8 PLATES IN COLOUR*
*AND*
*19 ILLUSTRATIONS IN*
*BLACK & WHITE*

COLLINS · 14 ST. JAMES'S PLACE · LONDON
MCMXLVII

PRODUCED BY
ADPRINT LIMITED LONDON

PRINTED IN GREAT BRITAIN
BY JARROLD AND SONS LTD NORWICH
ON MELLOTEX BOOK PAPER MADE
BY TULLIS RUSSELL AND CO LTD MARKINCH SCOTLAND

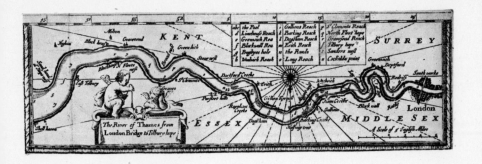

# LIST OF ILLUSTRATIONS

*PLATES IN COLOUR*

# BLACK AND WHITE ILLUSTRATIONS

THE CITY OF LONDON SEEN THROUGH AN ARCH OF WESTMINSTER BRIDGE
Wash drawing by Antonio Canale, called Canaletto, 1747

# INTRODUCTION

IN the amount and magnificence of her trade, London surpasses all her predecessors in whatever period of history we like to choose. Whether it is Tyre or Venice, Hamburg or Rotterdam, they all conducted a trade small in proportion to that which is centred on London to-day.

Most of the great ports of the world owe their commercial success to the geographical position they command, but apart from this particular advantage, London possesses many others equally desirable in a port. First there is her position in relation to the other great ports of the world, which cannot be equalled. Secondly, the disposition of her people has through every age been inclined towards sea-trade with other countries, an essential factor in the development of a port. But London is unique, for in addition to being the capital of England, and the British Empire, she has to-day sixty-nine miles of tideway whose expediency for the interchange of goods remains unparalleled. London owes her greatness to these waters which the Venerable Bede in the year A.D. 605 described as a "market for many nations repairing to them by land and sea."

The fact of London being the capital city and having a population of over eight millions often overshadows the supreme importance she holds in the commercial world. For when we think of London many of us think simply of Buckingham Palace or the Houses of Parliament, but to this we ought to add the distinction of being the greatest port in the world. The Port of London is like the human heart with the Thames serving the dual purpose of veins and arteries. Every flood tide gives a new beat of life to Britain and the Empire, for up its grey and muddy waters come the ships of all nations laden with every cargo imaginable. Whether it is wool from Australia or mutton from New Zealand, timber from Canada or petroleum from Persia —they are all brought to-day to the docks which spread snakelike from the Tower to Tilbury and every ebb sees these same ships sailing north, south, east, and west with cargoes from our own industries.

To obtain a true picture of the Port in all its aspects, its commercial importance, its romantic history, and last but by no means least, its beauty, which is so little known, we must start at the beginning.


## EARLY HISTORY OF THE PORT

IN the first days there was little question of trade anywhere, and the Celts laid the first foundations of London solely because of the natural advantages of the position. They are said to have given the charming name of "Llyn-Din," Celtic for the "hill by the pool," to what can have been little more than a collection of mud huts. Although in A.D. 61 Tacitus described London as "a colony much frequented by merchants and trading vessels," it is not till Alfred comes to the throne in the ninth century that we see the real genesis of the Port of London.

The history of our land is punctuated by certain sovereigns who did more to encourage new and ambitious projects than any who came after them. Of these King Alfred and Queen Elizabeth, the Virgin Queen, shine out above all others. Having obtained information about the Baltic, Alfred subsidised expeditions to Scandinavia; he made laws protecting merchants arriving from abroad, and thus increased the volume of trade brought to our shores. His improvements in ship-building and his interest in the arts of navigation gave encouragement to merchants and sailors alike. It is interesting to think that from the same upper reaches where Alfred first built his galleys for the protection of the kingdom, many of the "little ships" sailed on their maiden voyages a thousand years later, and ultimately won glory in the fight against the Axis Powers.

At first the scale of the Port was very small, the biggest ships being about one hundred tons. These used to lie at moorings in the centre of the river, while their cargo was unloaded into barges, which could not have been much larger than ordinary rowing-boats. At certain places on the northern shores "hythes," or small harbours, had been constructed. The only two of any real importance were Queenhythe and Billingsgate, between which there grew up a keen rivalry for predominance in the English trade.

THE THAMES FROM RICHMOND HOUSE

Oil painting by Antonio Canale, called Canaletto, 1746

THE ITALIAN BRIDGE CONNECTING BRIDEWELL AND BLACKFRIARS AT THE ENTRANCE TO THE FLEET RIVER

Oil painting by Samuel Scott, 1710-1772

A distinction between the Pool (that part of the river lying immediately below London Bridge) and the upper reaches of the Port is made apparent with the opening of the first stone London Bridge in 1209. This was by no means the first bridge to span the Thames, but hitherto each one had been made of wood and fell into disrepair so often that the Corporation was finally prevailed upon to build one of stone.

For those early days, the bridge of Peter the Chaplain of Colechurch was a tremendous achievement, but its design had certain unforeseen consequences. With great difficulty nineteen piers, or "sterlings" as they were called, had been sunk into the river bed, and built up to support the bridge; each of these was twenty feet wide and proved such an obstruction to the river that there was an appreciable difference between the level of the water on each side of the bridge; the blocking of one of the arches with a water-wheel aggravated this effect even more, and caused such rapids that the passage through the bridge was dangerous for all but the most skilful watermen.

The shops and houses which lined its whole length, the chapel of St. Thomas, and the barges shooting the rapids must have increased the excitement and fascination that the Pool held for any watchful observer. Due to the advantages which the bridge afforded, the Port soon spread to the Surrey shore, thus dispersing a large quantity of the merchandise that was already threatening to swamp the small hythes of the City. Another consequence of this work was the final death of Queenhythe, which lay above the Pool, as a hythe of any great importance; for after the bridge had been open some years, it was found that the inconvenience of waiting for the drawbridge to open was too much for the peace of mind of any captain; also as ships increased in size, the passage through the arches became so hazardous that Queenhythe gradually became the centre of all the small up-river traffic, and Billingsgate the chief market for foreign trade. To-day, Billingsgate, though she has lost the wealth and glamour of her foreign merchandise, still retains some of her past glory in being the foremost fish market of England.

Now, when we lean over London Bridge and gaze down into the murky depths which swirl beneath us, we find it difficult to think that this same water, only a hundred years ago, gave up a rich harvest. The muddy stream which moves tirelessly up the sixty-nine miles from Southend to Teddington was once a fishful river: up till the war of 1914, flounders were still being caught near Brentford; in 1920 my sister caught a trout with a toy fishing-net off Chiswick Eyot, where now it is difficult to find even a stickleback. As late as the eighteenth century, the water between Deptford and London was fished by more than eight hundred Londoners; the tug-masters and watermen of to-day little realise that up those same reaches which they know so well—Bugsby's and Blackwall, Greenwich and Lime-house—now such a mixture of smuts and smells, Londoners once dragged

9

their nets. Roach, plaice, smelt, flounders, salmon, eels, gudgeon, dabs and haddock were all caught there in abundance.

But it was in the age of Elizabeth that the star of British commerce came really into the ascendant. Just as Alfred laid a sure foundation for trade, so Elizabeth built the first storey of the great structure which stands to-day. No other sovereign worked so hard to develop the nation's influence abroad, and to promote the aggrandisement of her people in the New World through the medium of sea-power. She was ably assisted by her secretary, Cecil, and the skilful financier and commercial genius, Sir Thomas Gresham. Cecil organised the expeditions which were now sent out to seek the New World, led by the men whose immortal names we know so well—Frobisher to Hudson's Bay in 1576, Gilbert to Newfoundland in 1583, and Hawkins to Puerto Rico early in 1572; Lancaster sailed four times to the east and Raleigh discovered the gold mines of the Orinoco in his attempt to find El Dorado. The imagination of every young man was fired by these exploits which inspired them to travel abroad and exploit what they discovered for the benefit of England. Just before this era, the Russian Company had been formed by Sebastian Cabot, after an unsuccessful attempt to find the North-East passage to India. This led to a large increase of trade with Russia and, encouraged by Elizabeth, four other companies were started. They were the Levant, the African, the Virginian, and lastly, but of far the greatest importance, the East India Company.

Prosperity is incompatible with war, for trade and peace walk hand in hand. The truth of this was known to Gresham; and the occupation of the Low Countries by the Spaniards gave him ample opportunity to exalt London at the expense of Antwerp. Religious persecution by the Spaniards compelled thousands of Netherlanders to seek refuge in England and many of these fugitives were bankers who, fearing that they would lose all if they remained in their own country, deposited their riches in London banks. Gresham had foreseen this, and did everything in his power to facilitate the influx of foreign wealth, so that within a few years London was the banking centre of the world. Later he was able by skilful negotiation to use much of this money as capital to finance the enterprises of his Queen.

This was not all, for the general exodus from the Low Countries included a large number of artisans of all trades who, on fleeing the country, set up shop in London. The downfall of Antwerp was complete when, in 1585, the Spaniards sacked and destroyed the city, and all its trade was inveigled into the Port of London by the ingenious Gresham. Elizabeth made London's position doubly sure by withdrawing all the privileges of the Hanseatic League and ordering the Mayor of London to shut the Steelyard, the headquarters of the German merchants in the City. Thus London came to hold the wealth of the world in her hand and, though many envious eyes have since been cast upon her, she has managed to breast the flood tide of all opposition and win for herself the position she holds to-day.

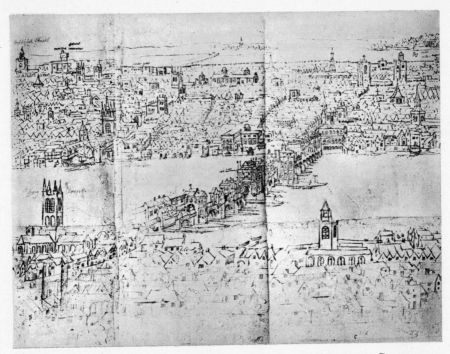

## FROM LEGAL QUAYS TO THE FIRST DOCKS

UP till the sixteenth century Billingsgate and Queenhythe had been able to absorb the whole trade of the Port. But in the latter part of Elizabeth's reign it had increased so greatly that wharves and warehouses in many other parts of the Pool began to be used. This practice gave such opportunities for smuggling and the evasion of customs duties by "greedy persons," as Elizabeth termed them, that she instituted the Legal Quays. Despite it being obvious from the very start that this was a highly impracticable scheme, Elizabeth decreed that merchandise could not be unloaded at any quays other than the twenty recognised by her. Each of these was situated on the north bank, and having a total frontage of only 1,419 feet, they were always overcrowded with an excessive amount of goods. The owners of these quays were quick to realise the controlling position in which they had been placed by th Queen, and used it to their own advantage, and to the general distress of the merchants. By charging exorbitant rates, and by successfully opposing all those who stood before them, they became monopolists of the worst kind. These quays were the root of the evil which slowly reduced the Port to a state of utmost depravity; for crime throve and continued unchecked till 1801 when the first Thames police force was formed.

There was as yet no official administration of the river, and those in power turned a deaf ear to the pleadings of both merchants and captains of ships; although the vested interests in the Legal Quays were many, this deplorable situation was mainly due to the indifference of Parliament and the City Corporation. Both bodies recognised that the Port was being ruined at the country's expense, but as no charter had ever placed the onus of the welfare of the Port in the hands of any particular body, both considered that they were absolved from all blame.

Before we see the depths to which the administration of the Port sank, and the extent to which the depredations rose, we must first review the three most disastrous years in the history of London: that the events of these years did not prove fatal is remarkable.

In 1665 the Great Plague with a single blow brought all traffic to a standstill and put the Port out of action. In addition the Dutch, eager to win back their former position in world trade, were hammering at our front door and blockading the river. In the next year the Great Fire, starting in Pudding Lane, swept unchecked from the Tower to Temple Church. In its path were left the charred timbers of 13,200 houses, the smoking ruins of every wharf and warehouse on the north bank, and the smouldering ruins of £10,000,000 worth of merchandise. In consequence of the fire an opportunity to rebuild London, more beautiful than ever before, was given above all to Sir Christopher Wren and Inigo Jones. This, as we know, they were not slow to seize, and it is only to be hoped that to-day equal advantage will be reaped from the terrible fire of 29th December 1940, which, though shorter in duration, burned with far greater intensity than that of 1666.

1667 saw the greatest threat that we have ever had of invasion, greater even than that following the evacuation of the B.E.F. from Dunkirk in 1940. The Dutch sailed up the Medway and, having blown up the fort at Sheerness, burned a number of the King's ships at Chatham. While one half of their fleet was employed on this operation, the other sailed up the Thames. In the Lower Hope they were stopped by a bridge of barges which had been thrown across the river for the easy passage of troops and material. It is curious how history repeats itself, for some of the anti-invasion precautions taken during 1940 were just as capricious as those of 1667. Pepys in his diary deplores the impetuosity of certain officers who, when ordered to sink two ships in the hope of blocking the river against the enemy fleet, chose an East Indiaman, only recently arrived in port with an £80,000 cargo aboard, and a naval auxiliary full of supplies. In 1940 the Lower Hope was once more closed to the invader, but by a boom of

THE LANDING-STAGE AT LAMBETH PALACE IN THE SEVENTEENTH CENTURY
Drawing by Wenceslaus Hollar, 1607–1677

stronger material than that of 1667, and one which would have incurred no adverse criticism from Pepys.

Peace was made in the same year and England turned eagerly to the task of reasserting herself and strengthening her position in the commercial world, a position which France, as well as Holland, was now threatening. For during the war France, under the shrewd guidance of Colbert, had been steadily building up her wealth with new industries. During the same period there was relatively little development in our own economic position: in 1662 our imports were valued at £4,016,019 as against £4,196,140 for 1668; our exports for the earlier year had been £2,022,812 in comparison with £2,063,275 six year later.

However, one of England's rivals was eliminated when Louis XIV hoisted France with the petard of papism, by revoking the Edict of Nantes. Since 1598 this Edict had granted religious toleration to the Huguenots, who were the most industrious and skilful artisans in France. By annulling this order Louis dealt an irreparable blow to the great financial system which Colbert had worked so hard to set up. The immediate result was a welcome exodus from France to England of 700,000 goldsmiths, silversmiths, watchmakers and, what was most important of all, men skilled in the manufacture of silk, which had previously been imported from France.

Thus the balance of trade, which for three years had been weighted heavily against England, slowly readjusted itself in her favour. Having weathered disease and fire at home and foreign competition abroad, the

13

only obstacles to the prosperity of the Port were the irresponsibility of Parliament and the monopoly of the Legal Quay owners.

In 1721, Sir Robert Walpole took the reins and began his twenty-one years' Ministry, outstanding for the impetus it gave to commerce. Walpole was a firm believer in Free Trade, and his first success was to withdraw the export duty from one hundred and six articles of British manufacture, and the import duty from thirty-eight. This brought a large amount of new trade to Britain and facilitated commercial intercourse throughout the world. He next tried to introduce the bonded warehouse into British commerce, a move which would have provided a healthy stimulus to London's foreign trade if it had been successful. But so great was the furore which arose as a result of his proposals, particularly from the vested interests which they threatened, that Parliament refused to countenance them. Notwithstanding this failure there was a general advance in trade in the next fifty years and the number of ships based on the Port increased steadily. But this, although good in itself, only tended to aggravate the congestion of the river; for the Port was still stifled by the Legal Quays, which, through having to serve a larger number of ships, were in a far worse condition than before.

In 1705 the merchants of the Port had forwarded a written plea to Parliament complaining of their treatment by the Legal Quay owners and the iniquity of the whole system. They pointed out that the present state of affairs was losing to Bristol and other ports a large volume of trade which had previously come to London: secondly, that although Bristol's trade was far smaller, she had a quay frontage of 4,000 ft. compared with the 1,419-ft. frontage of London. They admitted that the Legal Quays had been augmented to a small extent by the Sufferance Wharves (the Sufferance Wharves were so termed because the permission granted to their owners to land goods there was liable to be taken away at short notice), but their owners had soon become as rapacious in enforcing their monopoly as those of the Legal Quays. The remonstrance had no effect, and both Parliament and the City Corporation maintained the same stubborn and obscurantist attitude of a hundred years before.

But this was by no means the only trouble, for the character of the Port in the eighteenth century and the circumstances in which trade was conducted were such that it is hard to see how the country prospered at all.

Ships still for the most part lay at moorings in the middle of the river, but these were nothing like sufficient to accommodate the increased traffic. Moreover, owing to the time taken to discharge goods into lighters, and then on to the Legal Quays, many ships remained at moorings for months at a time. Sometimes there were as many as seven hundred and seventy-five ships in the Port at once, all lying in "trots" of three or four ships deep, and extending as far down as Deptford. That captains managed to navigate their ships in such congested waters, and round the long meanders of the

TROOPS CROSSING THE THAMES FROM GRAVESEND TO TILBURY FORT
Coloured engraving published by F. West, c. 1785

Thames, is amazing. As there was no authority in the Port, ships arriving in the Pool moored where they liked, regardless of whether they were causing an obstruction to other ships or overloading a particular set of moorings. When merchandise was eventually landed, it was stored so openly and in such large quantities, owing to the inadequacy of the warehousing arrangements, that riverside gangs immediately banded together and carried out their villainy with unparalleled brazenness and audacity. They were helped in their nefarious occupation by the practice of using wharves as markets instead of purely for transit purposes. The position was not improved by the Revenue and Customs staff, who were so badly organised that some had no work at all, while others had so much that they could cope with none of it with proper efficiency. But this in actual fact did not affect the country as much as might be supposed, for the whole service was inordinately corrupt, and every official considered himself so underpaid that each took what he was pleased to call his "perquisites" from the hands of the "River Pirates."

These were the most villainous of the river rogues, being generally armed and equipped with their own boats. During the day they marked out the richest vessel in port, and then cut her adrift at dead of night. They then followed her till she ran aground, and they were able to pillage her at their own convenience. At dawn they deposited the spoil with "receivers," of whom there were many on the river bank.

15

The next most pernicious band, in order of villainy, were the "Night Plunderers." These were organised in gangs known as "Light Horsemen," and were made up of Coopers, Watermen, and Lumpers, all of whom were adept in their own particular form of crime. Having first picked their victim, they went aboard armed with crowbars, shovels and sacks. First the Lumpers unstowed the casks, which were generally filled with sugar, the most valuable commodity at that time, then the Coopers opened them, and lastly the Watermen filled the sacks. These, when full, contained one hundred pounds and were called Black Strap, for they were dyed black to make them less easily visible at night. The value of one night's haul was seldom less than £150. In addition to casks of sugar, they broached barrels of rum and drew the spirit off into skins with the help of special funnels. No doubt it sounds incredible that these men were able to work with such freedom while the captain and crew were on board. The fact is, that in most cases, nearly everyone was implicated in the crime except the captain, and the mate was heavily bribed to be sleeping soundly when the raid took place. The ships which were pillaged in this way were designated as "Game Ships," and were generally in the proportion of one ship of every four in port. The picture which the "Heavy Horsemen," or "Day Plunderers," presented must have been highly amusing, even if at the expense of the Port. For the "Heavy Horsemen" dressed themselves in an underdress known as a "jemmy," which had pockets before and behind, and round their legs they tied pouches and bags. Into these they slipped quantities of sugar, coffee, cocoa, ginger, and pimento during the course of the day's work.

The most despicable of the riverside fraternity were the "Mudlarks." These were men of the lowest order, who prowled about in the mud under the bow of any ship that was known to be "game," on the pretence of grubbing for jetsam. At a convenient moment their accomplices on board, usually Lumpers, handed down bags of sugar and other articles which the Mudlarks bore away to receivers.

The temptation for quick and easy gain spread to many civil professions. The rat-catchers were the most cunning and shameless of these land-sharks. Many ships at this time were infested with rats, and rat-catchers were therefore always given authority to come and go as they pleased on board all ships. They made it their custom to set their traps at night, and dishonoured their business by making each trip to and from the shore the opportunity for enriching themselves with plunder. Occasionally they resorted to the dastardly practice of introducing rats into ships, so that their services would be required still more.

This was the state of the Port up till the close of the century. The net result of all the depredations was an average annual loss of £800,000 by the Public Revenue and London Merchants, which passed into the pockets of the Light Horsemen and their colleagues.

VIEW OF ST. PAUL'S FROM LONDON BRIDGE, 1802
Coloured engraving by N. R. Black after J. C. Stadler

THE SHOT TOWER, WHARVES AND BREWERY BELOW WATERLOO BRIDGE

Coloured aquatint by G. Hunt after F. C. Turner, 1836

The commercial community had been agitated by this appalling situation for a long time, but could still get no satisfaction from their repeated pleadings to Parliament. Now, however, we see the death of the Legal Quays, and the construction of the first docks, through the energy and persistence of one man.

This was Mr. William Vaughan, a London merchant. Having written a series of treatises advocating the construction of wet docks and warehouses in 1793, he convened a meeting of all the merchants in the Port of London in March of the next year. A petition to Parliament followed, in which the whole problem was reviewed, the causes for the Port's debility were analysed, and the improvements necessary for its recovery recommended. Parliament's eyes were at last opened to the seriousness of the position and they began immediately to discuss the various suggestions made by Vaughan and his committee. Of these we need only be concerned with two. First, a plan which was never adopted, but which is interesting nevertheless for its ambitious and imaginative character. This was originated by Mr. Reveley, who suggested that the present channel of the Thames should be straightened by cutting a canal across the bends of the river, and the area thus saved be converted into docks. Reveley intended that the first canal should cut across the Isle of Dogs, and that a second continue over Blackwall Point, coming out into the Thames at the bottom of Bugsby's Reach. When completed, the plan was to transform Bugsby's and Blackwall, Greenwich and Limehouse Reaches into one vast dock area. Thereby the long journey round the Isle of Dogs, which in a sailing-ship was always full of difficulty and worry for a captain, would be eliminated. Though highly enterprising, this scheme did not solve the tidal problem, and was anyhow too costly to be considered seriously.

The second scheme was put forward by the Merchants of the West India Company and provided for the making of two parallel docks across the Isle of Dogs, from Limehouse to Blackwall, and these in fact since their opening in 1802 have been the West India Docks. Part of Reveley's scheme was realised later by the making of a canal across the Isle of Dogs, and directly south of the docks, which eventually became the third or "South" Dock. After a long struggle between the conflicting interests of the committee, the second scheme was finally decided upon and received the Royal Assent in the July of 1799.

Another great reform was made, in 1801, by Mr. Patrick Colquhoun, who persuaded the West India Company to appoint a police force on the Thames. Through him a headquarters was set up at Wapping. Constables were enrolled and acted as watchmen on board each ship, and had authority to search all labourers when they returned home in the evening. The indignation which the institution of this force aroused among the whole coterie of river robbers was so great that on one occasion an attack was made on the headquarters, and the mob was only dispersed with the help of firearms. But the force achieved an instantaneous success, and the "perquisites," which had made life comparatively easy for hundreds of rogues, now began to reach their rightful owners.

The foundation stone of the West India Docks was laid on 12th July 1800. The ceremony was carried out with much pomp and splendour and the day was treated as a national holiday. With the actual construction of the five great docking systems which to-day handle the majority of the trade of the Port, we need not concern ourselves here; but a little should be said of the details of the West India Docks, for they were the first of their kind, and formed the basis for all other projects.

As has already been stated, the West India Docks were to consist of two parallel docks. One was for the import trade and the other for export, but both were of the same dimensions, being 2,600 ft. long and 450 ft. broad, inter-connected at one end by a basin. Particular regard was paid to the construction of sufficient warehousing accommodation. To the north, east, and west of the Import Quay five-storey warehouses were built, a number of which would still be standing to-day had it not been for the blitz; to the south there were sheds and vaults assigned purely for the stowage of rum. The Export Dock was comparatively free of buildings, for goods were usually brought alongside by carts or lighters and loaded aboard at once. Of cranes there were none as we know them to-day, goods being loaded with the aid of small winches, and the help of block and tackle.

The West India Docks, when finished, won renown throughout the world; the lassitude which had stifled the Port for so long had at last been replaced by the energy of a more enlightened age. On 22nd August 1802 the docks were opened in the presence of the Prime Minister, Henry Addington, and the first ship to sail into the thirty-acre lake was appropriately one bearing his name, and flying the "flags of all nations," to mark the international spirit in which the docks had been built.

The realising of Walpole's dream by the passing of the Warehousing Act, in 1803, gave the necessary *élan* to the march of reform which now began, and which did not halt till 1886, when it reached Tilbury.


## THE DOCKS

THE year 1800 marks the beginning of a most dramatic era, a century of reform and progress. The industrial revolution demanded a new attitude of mind, a reversal of the old policy of *laissez faire*. On the green hills factories sprouted, and appeased their rapacious appetites with raw material transported in English ships driven for the first time with English coal. As industry developed and our mercantile fleet increased in size and numbers, the need for proper facilities, whereby commerce could be efficiently transacted, became self-evident. Although Parliament had up

THE OLD CUSTOM HOUSE
Coloured engraving by T. Bowles, 1753

till now turned a blind eye to the throttling of trade within the Port, the immediate success of the West India system soon cleared its vision. From now on it was realised that the only way in which the increasing volume of goods could be efficiently handled was by the construction of wet docks. Stimulated by the example of the West India merchants, new companies were formed, and charters granted to them by Parliament for the construction of docks and warehouses. But although by 1900 the results of their enterprise could be seen stretching from the Tower to Tilbury, the evolution of the five great docking systems was accompanied by a complete cycle in the fortunes of the Port. For in the execution of their plans and in their attitude to the many existing interests within the Port, the Dock Companies showed a narrow-mindedness which only experience could alter. Disputes broke out between them and the various riverside parties; the old Legal Quay owners complained that their businesses would be ruined by the docks, while the lightermen said that the demand for their services would not only die out, but that the dues, charged by the Companies for lighters wishing to enter a dock and load up with cargo, were prohibitive. This dispute was quickly settled by Parliament, which realised that some form of compensation was due; they therefore inserted in every Dock Act a Free Water clause, stipulating that in future no charges could be made, and that the water inside every dock was to be "free."

The ensuing competition and lack of co-operation between these rival concerns increased the difficulties of the Port. Finally, the City Corporation, to whom Richard II had entrusted the authority for the proper administration of the Thames, failed to carry out the day-to-day upkeep of the Port. The result was that by the middle of the century, in spite of the West and East India Docks, the London and St. Katharine's and part of the Surrey Commercial system, the Port was once more in a bad way. Owing to the negligence of the Corporation the river was silting up, and when reproached by Parliament they attempted to divert the charge on to Trinity House. But although the Elder Brethren had been given the right of selling sand dredged from the river bed, as ballast, their responsibility lay only, as it does to-day, in the lighting and buoying of channels and in the examination of prospective pilots. Furthermore, the City Councillors had failed to enlarge the mooring system to serve the increased traffic, and consequently many of the largest ships refused to come farther than the Isle of Dogs, for fear of running onto a sandbank. After a Parliamentary inquiry in 1857 this situation was eased slightly by the formation of the Thames Conservancy Board. Under their management the Port for a few years breathed freely again. Buoys were laid, the channel was dredged regularly and piers and landing-places were built. This spring-cleaning revitalised trade but proved the undoing of a number of the private companies. Many of these found that, as trade increased, it was either to their

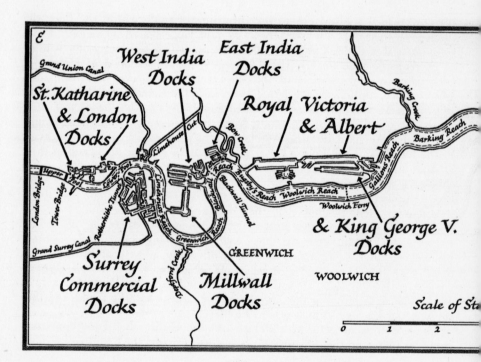

advantage to combine with one of their rivals, or that they were forced to such an expedient in order to survive at all. So throughout the century we see a slow and painful process of amalgamation.

As early as 1838 the India Companies realised that each could benefit from the other, and they therefore combined to capture the monopoly of the West and East Indian trade, which was at that time the most valuable in the world. But it was in 1864 that the largest fusion was made. This was precipitated by the opening of the Victoria Dock in 1855 which completely revolutionised the loading and discharge of ships. The efficiency of this system caused the London and St. Katharine Docks to lose so much of their trade that they were left with no alternative but to combine with the Victoria Company. On the south bank of the river, the four independent concerns trading to Scandinavian countries became the single Surrey Commercial Docks Company. In 1880 the original plan of the Victoria Dock was completed by the addition of the Royal Albert; this dock, despite its length of one and three-quarter miles, was one of the cheapest ever built and for facilities was as yet unsurpassed. Meanwhile, as a result of the opening of the Suez Canal, and the diversion of a large amount of their trade to Mediterranean ports, the profits of the East and West India Company had fallen sharply; moreover the opposition of the Wharfingers

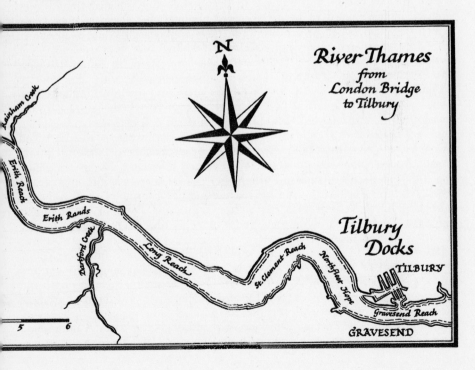

DOCKS AND WAREHOUSES OF THE WEST INDIA COMPANY ON THE ISLE OF DOGS
Coloured lithograph by William Daniell, 1802

and Lightermen, arising from the protection given them by the Free Water clause, had increased alarmingly. In desperation they opened the Tilbury system. This proved to be an absolute bugbear, for the passenger trade which they had hoped to capture from their opponents did not materialise. Unable even to pay their expenses over the first year they realised their defeat, and under pressure from Parliament formed a joint committee with the London and St. Katharine Dock Companies in 1887.

This compromise could never have been successful, for the London Company, holding three-quarters of the shares, was completely arbitrary as to the measures which it adopted. Holding such a large proportion of the capital, they advocated and could afford a ca'canny policy, whereas the East and West India Company knew, from their wide experience of administration, that such a scheme was madness. With trade falling and dissension among the different parties growing, Parliament realised that in addition to over-expansion the Port was suffering from a lack of central control and firm administration. It is ironical that after a hundred years of development the Port should be paralysed once more, not this time by a shortage but by a surfeit of docking space.

In 1900 a Royal Commission was appointed to look into the whole question and to recommend a system whereby disaster might be averted and the prosperity of the Port restored. As a result of their inquiry, and after some eight years of wrangling and indecision in the House, a single new authority was formed for the purpose of administering, preserving and improving the Port of London. For although the Royal Commission attacked the problem conscientiously and energetically, their example was

LONDON DOCKS
Coloured aquatint by D. Havell after H. Haseler, 1816

not emulated by Parliament, and it was only after Mr. Lloyd George had successfully propitiated the various factions within the Port that his successor, Mr. Winston Churchill, was able in 1908 to secure the passage of the Port of London Act. By this measure the Port of London Authority was constituted and became responsible for the welfare and administration of the Port, which was defined as stretching from Teddington to a point just beyond the Nore Lightship. The Thames Conservancy Board was relegated to administering the river above Teddington. The Royal Assent was given in the face of much opposition from those who no longer believed in the construction of docks, but favoured riverside quays or "cuts" instead; however, Mr. Lloyd George decided correctly that docks were the only practicable scheme for a port such as London. The reasons are many, but the overriding factor is the tide. In a port where the rise and fall is only a few feet, such as Antwerp or Hamburg, Glasgow or Avonmouth, unloading at riverside jetties is easy and satisfactory; but in London a fast tide, an average rise and fall of twenty feet, and the wide dispersal of warehouse accommodation make this quite impossible.

Ever since the 31st March 1909 the Port of London Authority have been one of the public utility services of the country. Independent of the Government, and completely non-profit-making, their avowed aim is to further London's international trade by providing, from the dues collected, facilities advantageous to commerce. Of the twenty-eight members on the board, eighteen are elected by the shipowners, merchants, and other payers of dues; the remaining ten are the appointed representatives of the Admiralty, Ministry of Transport, L.C.C., Trinity House and the City

23

Corporation. The P.L.A. have received little acknowledgment and few words of thanks for their great achievement in putting the Port on its feet again; indeed the importance and perfection of the Port of London is hardly realised even by the citizens of London; but for this they are hardly to be blamed for, lying below Tower Bridge and bordered on all sides by forbidding walls and warehouses, the Port is inaccessible to the general public, and remains concealed even from those in the pleasure steamers bound for Greenwich or Gravesend.

Dockland is a unique part of London possessing a romance and fascination particular to itself, the accumulation of centuries of ceaseless association with ships and those who sail in them. To-day the riverside is not darkened by a tracery of masts and spars, and the exquisite but indefinable music of ropes moving through their blocks is seldom heard; but if the iron men of old could accompany us on a tour of the forty-four miles of quays and docks, they might well be satisfied with the fruits of their legacy.

Nearest to the City, and nestling beneath the whitey-grey battlements of the Tower of London, lie the St. Katharine Docks, whose walls are black and gloomy in contrast; but behind this rough exterior there is a story as bright and colourful as the Arabian Nights. Once through the gates, one is struck by the miniature and old-world quality of the whole system. Planned roughly in the shape of a letter E, it comprises two small docks bounded on nearly every side by warehouses built close to the dockside. During the war the warehouses bordering the Eastern Docks were destroyed in the great blitz on the docks of 7th September 1940, a night that is well remembered by all those who were on duty there; as the flames caught hold, the air became heavy with the fumes of the brandy, cinnamon and nutmeg which were stored inside. However, half the warehouses are still standing and guard a variety of goods. Of greatest interest is the ivory "floor," where we see rows of tusks, or teeth as they are called in the trade, laid out for view. Each one bears its own specifications relating to weight, the ship it came in, and any damage which it incurred during transit. Some of these show that their original owners suffered severely from toothache for in an attempt to relieve the irritation they have worn, by constant rubbing, deep grooves in the offending tusks.

On the top floor rum is being bottled, corked and labelled, and in another wing "spirit proofs" are being taken by Customs officials. Each puncheon is opened by one of the P.L.A.'s coopers, and a small amount of spirit withdrawn; then with the aid of a specific-gravity measure the proof is taken and the merchant informed of the degree of dilution necessary before he can put his spirit on the market. Here, in an atmosphere which makes our nostrils quiver, we see that goods are "worked" by labour supplied for the merchant by the P.L.A. For the Authority's work does not end with the provision of docks and warehouses, but goes one step farther and furnishes merchants and shipowners with the services of a large staff of

St. Katharine Docks
Coloured lithograph by J. Phelps after W. Ranwell, 1828

experts. In this way every conceivable form of cargo is inspected and handled by specialists, who have devoted their lives to particular spheres of trade. So great is the reputation of these men for sound discrimination that their advice is highly valued and their judgment is never questioned. This unique service of the Port of London, originated and scrupulously maintained by the P.L.A., is partly responsible for the international popularity of the port with merchants.

Continuing our tour we come to the tortoise-shell floor, which is covered with neat piles of "Hawkshell Turtle." Each one consists of thirteen pieces which are divided into "shell, underbelly, and hoof"; the laborious work of sorting the contents of each crate into individual "fish" by the size, shape, and colour of the shell is yet another example we find in these docks of the amazing variety of the P.L.A.'s work. As we leave the St. Katharine Docks, we are told that, for many years past, the difficulties of manœuvring modern steamships within their tiny space have necessitated the exotic cargoes of ivory, spices, wine, and curios being lightered to them from the lower reaches.

25

Next door the London Docks, although twenty years older than the St. Katharine system, can still harbour ships of four thousand tons, and always present a busy scene. The general air of activity is increased by the discharging of goods into lighters as well as on to the dockside, depending on whether they are to be placed in bond or shipped to a private warehouse up-river. Such is the case at the Western Dock, which is lined by trim cargo vessels, whose derricks weave backwards and forwards to the puffings and protests of hard-worked winches. The barges, which besiege every ship like piglets round a sow, are in strict contrast, for over these there is a general air of tranquillity and silence, which may be one of the reasons for their being so aptly christened "dumb" lighters.

The London Docks are probably most renowned for their wool stores which before the war housed over 200,000 bales. Only two of the nine warehouses escaped being blasted or totally destroyed in the blitz, but these provide sufficient temporary storage space, and still enable merchants to sample wool under the best conditions. For wool is best viewed away from the sun, and in the northern light of these showrooms the respective merits of each of the three hundred and fifty varieties of wool can be seen to advantage. Each bale measures six feet by four feet and weighs six hundred pounds; on arrival in the warehouse they are stacked neatly by a man driving a piling-machine. This fascinating and ingenious invention is a good example of the labour-aiding innovations which have been introduced by the P.L.A.; it resembles a giant pair of mobile tongs which, when operated, can pick up a bale and deposit it where it is wanted without any trouble at all.

In addition to wool, the London Docks handle nearly all the wine and spirit orders of this country. On arrival, the P.L.A. undertake for a certain charge the responsibility of sorting these valuable shipments in their vast wine cellars, of which the Crescent Wine Vault is the most remarkable. Here in the eerie light of the half-dozen gas-jets responsible for preserving the wine at a constant temperature, hundreds of great puncheons lie at rest, maturing peacefully. The unbroken rows resemble the serried ranks of a mysterious army, a pre-natal army; platoons of sherry, port, and other wines, each vintage waiting for the day when it will reach perfection, and be delivered only to meet its inevitable fate. The atmosphere is indescribable, a combination of mystery and beauty, accentuated by the penetrating silence which is broken only by the hissing gas-jets. Delicate pillars, more in keeping with a cathedral, broaden out into crescent arches which support the low ceiling, and these, when seen from the centre of the chamber, exemplify symmetry and grace. Here, in the catacombs of London, merchants can leave their wine in bond till they have found a customer, or they can sample a vintage if they wish to make a purchase.

Two miles farther downstream the Isle of Dogs bends the river into a colossal U. Within its two arms lie the West India and Millwall Docks.

VIEW OF THE POOL FROM LONDON BRIDGE
Lithograph by M. Parrott, 1841

Alongside the Import Dock is the white hull of one of the banana boats, sailing between the West Indies and London. Her cargo is coming ashore on a conveyor belt which runs from the nearest warehouse down into the ship's hold, where it is fed by a gang of stevedores. As the green clusters pass slowly into the warehouse each one breaks a ray of light, actuated by a selenium cell, causing its number to be automatically recorded. Before leaving the belt the bad fruit is separated from the good, which is loaded into lorries lined with straw, or into the insulated railway wagons which have been run into the warehouse. In this trade it is essential that cargoes should be unloaded quickly and with minimum handling, and it is by introducing improvements such as conveyor belts and the selenium cell that the P.L.A. have so successfully achieved this aim; moreover, by providing every dock and warehouse with railway sidings, they have effectively eliminated many problems rising from the wide dispersal, and in some cases even remoteness, of the London docks. The West India system was badly hit during the war and many of the original five-storey warehouses were totally destroyed. This has resulted in the rum trade passing to the St. Katharine Docks, though the vast quantities of sugar, handled here since the opening of the docks in 1802, are stored in the few warehouses still standing, and in portable sheds. Near the South Dock we can see high orderly piles of timber. Overhead, powerful gantries move backwards and forwards picking up thin naked trunks of mahogany or lowering massive lengths of teak as easily as if they were bamboo shoots. Adjoining the West India Docks is the Millwall system, which specialises in grain. Dominating its single L-shaped dock is the largest granary in the Port, capable of sucking into its seemingly insatiable inside 60,000 tons of grain.

Due west and on the other bank of the river we can see the masts of ships in the Surrey Commercial Docks at Rotherhithe. The first of these was the Great Howland Dock built in 1696, but in those days it was only used as a safe anchorage for ships, and a convenient place in which to carry out repairs. Some of the names of the later docks, such as Norway, Russia, Canada, and Quebec, should give the layman a hint as to the nature of the trade they handle, for Rotherhithe has for centuries been the centre of the softwoods industry.

Eleven miles below Tower Bridge we come to the Royal Docks, unsurpassed in constructional perfection and the Port Authority's *chef-d'œuvre*. The P.L.A. feel particularly proud of the results of their work in this part of the Port, and justifiably so; their addition of the King George V Dock in 1921 to the Royal Victoria and Royal Albert gave London the largest single area of dock water in the world. Enclosing its two hundred and forty-six acres are eleven miles of quays equipped with the most modern warehouses, cranes, and transport facilities. Being the largest system in the Port, and available to ships of over thirty thousand tons, it is not surprising that the Royal Docks are the centre for all trade entering the Thames. But although ships carrying cargoes of every description are unloaded here, the predominant warehousing business of the Royal Docks is in meat, dairy produce, and tobacco; the various other commodities are either stored temporarily while awaiting dispatch inland, or are lightered to other docks and warehouses farther up-river. To store the vast shipments of Australian lamb, Argentine beef, and New Zealand butter, the P.L.A. have three cold-storage warehouses, each of which can preserve an average of 6,000 tons of frozen produce.

Although by far the oldest of the Royal trinity, the Victoria Dock, after its recent reconstruction, is the most notable example of how trade can be encouraged by modern methods of planning. Bordering the North Quay are five three-storey warehouses, which were completed in time to accommodate war material destined for the invasion of the Continent. A large number of the ships now alongside are in the tobacco trade; those nearest to us are from America, for they are unloading the 900-pound barrel-like hogsheads particular to that country. Each of these is rolled into one of the warehouses where it is weighed and examined by Customs officials. When a "hand" of leaves has been taken as a sample, the tobacco is re-crated and taken away to be stored in one of the "shell"-type warehouses. These, as their name implies, are of a particular kind and constructed specially for storing tobacco. Overhead cranes, capable of moving in any direction, place each hogshead in the "shell," where it remains in bond till a manufacturer or merchant is ready for delivery.

With the development of industry and the growth of competitive markets manufacturers gradually came to realise the advantages which the Port of London offered for quayside factories, where raw material could be received

BARGE YARD, GREENWICH
Water colour by Norman Janes, 1943

and the finished article could be exported without any intermediate handling. The best example of this form of expansion is the four grain mills
on the south side of the Royal Victoria, which are the property of private
companies. Here, cargoes of grain can be discharged direct from the ships'
holds into the silos, only to leave the dock in the form of flour or dog
biscuits.

If we walk down the Royal Victoria to where it joins the Royal Albert
we can see half a million tons of shipping lying stem to stern in orderly
array. Rising amid the forest of masts and derricks, the funnels and flags
of many companies and countries brighten with their colour a scene which
must impress the most impassive heart; among the Company flags, those
of the Blue Star, Cunard, Peninsular and Oriental, Royal Mail, and Shaw
Savill Lines are especially prominent.

Another fifteen miles down river brings us at last to Tilbury, the final
stage in our tour of the London docks. But Tilbury is no longer the white
elephant of former days, for although for geographical reasons it may never
be able to compete with Southampton and Liverpool, it is now the destination of many cargo-passenger liners plying to and from the Empire. The

floating landing-stage, opened in 1930 by Mr. Ramsay MacDonald, enables ships of thirty thousand tons to land passengers comfortably at any stage of the tide: hitherto liners had been obliged to anchor in midstream and carry out disembarkation in tenders, a method which always proved lengthy and unsatisfactory. During the war years the big ships were away trooping; but now they are back and we see once more in Tilbury Docks the tall yellow funnels of the Orient Company; the white hulls of the "Strath" boats; ships of the Bibby Rotterdam Lloyd, and many other famous lines.

We have so far said little about that noble institution, the Corporation of Trinity House. Originally a private association of mariners, they were given their first charter "for the relief, increase, and augmentation of the Shipping of this Realm of England" by Henry VIII in 1514. Since then they have been the supreme Lighthouse Authority for the United Kingdom. A second but no less important duty is the examination of pilots and the administration of their services.

London has of necessity a larger number of pilots than most ports, and they have their headquarters on the Royal Terrace Pier at Gravesend. Here the Ruler of Pilots—magnificent title—arranges for the safe arrival and departure of every ship, and is able to watch each one pass from the window of his office. Qualifications of the highest order are necessary to become a pilot: a Master Mariners' Ticket and a thorough knowledge of the whole Port being among them. Owing to the size of the Port of London pilotage here is different from that of most ports. Vessels coming up the English Channel bound for London, take on their first pilot off Dungeness, and he brings the ship as far as Gravesend; here the "river" pilot takes over, and is responsible for the safety of the ship as far as the dock entrance, where he is in his turn succeeded by the dock pilot; this man is sometimes known as the "mud" pilot and takes the ship through the lock and alongside the quay. The system whereby each man has his particular area and form of duty has contributed greatly to the efficiency and services of the Port of London.

After visiting the five great docking systems, it would not be unreasonable to think that we had seen the full extent of the P.L.A.'s commercial interests; but we should be wrong, for we are now led into a gloomy side street in Houndsditch, at the end of which we see the depressing façade of the Cutler Street warehouse. Built in 1782, it has survived the ravages of two great wars only to continue for the P.L.A. the work for which it was originally designed by the East India Company. Five storeys high, it is surrounded on all sides by City offices and the warehouses of private merchants; such a setting seems to give its sooty walls an atmosphere of foreboding. When, therefore, we enter this amazing treasure-chamber and see before our eyes the exotic produce of the Orient, the contrast leaves us breathless; we feel overwhelmed by the aura of richness and quality, colour and delicacy which arises from these floors, so long associated with priceless carpets, ostrich

UNLOADING ESPARTO GRASS, EAST INDIA DOCKS
Water colour by Norman Janes, 1946

feathers, Pekin china, Havana cigars, and a catalogue of equally sumptuous goods too long to list here. As an example of the particular interest attached to each commodity stored in Cutler Street, the carpet trade is outstanding.

Carpets come to Cutler Street from Turkey, Persia, India and China; brilliant in colour, fantastic in design, many are worked in silk and gold thread, others, such as those from China, are more simple but possess that thick velvety quality of pile. Each one is different from the next, and is priced principally on the closeness of the stitches and the particular use for which it is intended. Thus Persian rugs, having two hundred stitches to the square inch, combine the qualities of durability and beauty, and are judged to be the most valuable. These carpets are the work of individual families and each one is woven with a stitch peculiar to the village in which it is made. So intricate is each pattern, and so meticulous the blending of every hue, that many of those employed in this work are said to have gone blind at an early age. On arrival in England the carpets are often so sandy, from their passage across the desert in a camel caravan, that they have to be sent away to be washed, and are later inspected by the P.L.A. experts. If any damage has been incurred during transit the judgment given by the floor manager, as in every other branch of trade, is taken as final by merchant and insurance agent alike. Although London, and not Smyrna, is

31

now the centre of the carpet trade, the business is still largely carried on by Armenian merchants who, like those of every other country, recognise the advantages offered by the Port of London Authority for successful commercial transactions. Here at Cutler Street we end our tour of the Port and emerge still dazzled by the wealth of goods which we have seen, and more than ever impressed by the complexity of the Authority's work. That they are successful goes without saying, for within the first twenty-five years of their administration the total tonnage of goods dealt with increased by twenty-five per cent, and that of the ships entering and leaving the Port by nearly fifty per cent.

Since 1909, the P.L.A. has achieved an outstanding success in administration, yet this is almost overshadowed by the Port's magnificent record during the war. From the outbreak of hostilities its economic and strategic value made it a priority target of the *Luftwaffe*. For six years the Port was at action stations, and under attack from bombs, mines or rockets. The attacks on the docks started on 7th September 1940 with the largest daylight raid ever launched on London; this was followed by a systematic blitzing of the whole Port. High-explosive and incendiary bombs were not the only weapons used; magnetic and acoustic mines, and in the last nine months of the war the $V_1$ and $V_2$ all added to the difficulties and dangers of those fighting to keep the Port open. That in spite of the widespread destruction the Port was not completely dislocated, but continued to berth and unload ships, was due to the multiple efforts of the P.L.A., the civil defence services, and the Royal Navy. Sometimes, after an unusually heavy raid, the river was closed for a few hours to allow certain reaches to be swept for suspected mines, but apart from this the Port remained open and extended all its peace-time facilities to the national effort. However, London's position, though advantageous for trade in peace-time, now rendered her so vulnerable to air attack that only those ships engaged in feeding and arming the capital and south-eastern counties were allowed up the Thames, the majority being diverted to less exposed harbours.

During those years London River was an inspiring sight and a scene of immense activity. Despite the many charred shells of warehouses and the angry scars of devastation, the Port has never appeared so indomitable as it did then. Never before had the shipyards on the river bank been so loud with the clang of the riveter's hammer, nor so bright with the arc-welder's flame, for from their slips tank-landing craft began to take their first plunge. The Port within a few months had all the appearances of a naval base. Minesweepers swept the river as far west as Kew, and from even higher up the river the "little ships" came down to feel for the first time the lift of the open sea. Often on rounding Blackwall Point you could see a destroyer, corvette, or submarine steaming slowly up the river to refit in the East India Docks; farther downstream a cruiser was sometimes passed, bound for the Royal system, to undergo extensive repairs in one of the dry docks.

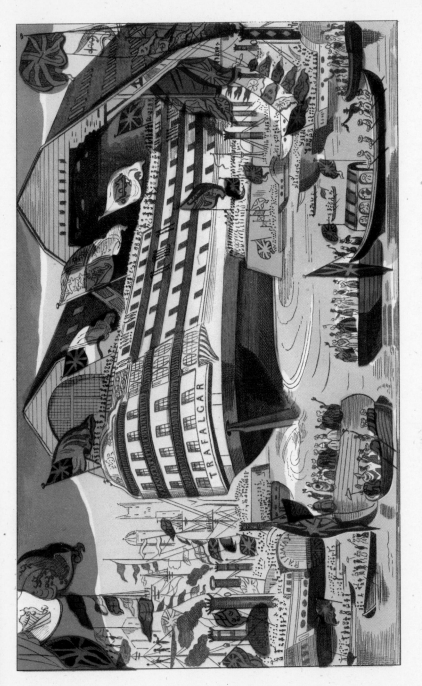

THE LAUNCHING OF H.M.S. 'TRAFALGAR' AT WOOLWICH, JUNE 1841

Coloured engraving by H. O. Minories from a Deptford scrapbook in the British Museum

THE GUN WHARF, TOWER OF LONDON
Oil painting by Henry Pether, 1863

Tilbury became a port in itself, for its commodious basin provided a comfortable berth for many of the patrol ships of the river, and its docks were in constant use for converting merchant ships, such as the *Rawalpindi* and *Jervis Bay*, into naval auxiliaries. At Southend the naval control station, situated at the end of the famous pier, marshalled the convoys in preparation for the dangerous run up the East Coast, or southwards through the Straits of Dover. Here in the estuary the battle was always liable to flare up suddenly, and the sky to become wreathed with vapour trails. Sea Reach saw many sad sights ships torpedoed in convoy being towed stern-first up-river to be patched together and sent to sea again; an oil tanker blowing up on a mine alongside the Thameshaven wharf, after surviving her perilous voyage across the Atlantic. Undaunted by events such as these, and in spite of the frequent air raids, ships were discharged and London was kept alive and free.

The Port had girded on its armour early in the war, but by 1943 it was mobilised for offensive action. As a result of secret works being undertaken, weird shapes began to appear in many parts of the Port. The Maunsell Bombardment Towers were towed forth from the Surrey Commercial Docks, where they had been built, and sunk on the Nore sands to resist aerial and sea attacks on the convoy rendezvous. The Maunsell project was distinctly Wellsian in appearance, for each of the seven octagonal towers stood on four stilt-like legs, and was connected to its fellows by cat-walks. At Gravesend other forts of a different design were constructed and then placed off the Kentish coast.

The Port of London's contribution to victory culminated in the "build-up" for the invasion of Normandy. Behind the virgin banks of the river the "Phoenix" began to rear its fantastic shape, and mystify everyone. At a certain stage in the work the river wall was cut away so that the giant caissons floated out into midstream, where they could be towed up to the King George V Dock for final completion. The Port can boast of having had a large interest in the Mulberry Harbour at Arromanches, for seventy-five per cent of the concrete work necessary for the construction of the formidable "Phoenix" was undertaken on Thames-side. But by far the strangest vessels ever seen in the Port were the three H.M.S. *Conundrums*, which carried part of the "Pluto" pipe-line across to France. These monstrous bobbins, each weighing two hundred and fifty tons, were built in one of the Tilbury dry docks, and later towed round the coast to prepare for the great enterprise that was to come; for these preparations were quickly recognised as being the prelude to some great new effort, though nobody knew where or when the blow was to be struck.

In May 1944 the tempo of work in the Port reached a tremendous pitch. Invasion barges steamed up the river by the score, and berthed at the special hards and ramps which had been constructed for them. Here the work of loading tanks and lorries was carried out with minimum delay. At the

Royal Docks war material arrived in increasing quantities from a seemingly inexhaustible source, and was loaded on to Liberty ships, which were then dispersed to different parts of the Port.

On 4th June the armada sailed; it consisted of 209 ships, of which 194 had been loaded in the London docks. In their wake went many of the humblest craft of London River—the dumb lighters. Determined not to be left behind, they had been converted into floating kitchens, petroleum tankers and store boats. Though somewhat out of place in the open sea, they made a gallant sight bobbing about off the Normandy beach-head clad in their white-and-blue camouflage, and were of inestimable service to many of the little ships. The Second Front marked the climax to the Port of London's spectacular war effort, and the successful defence of its supreme position. The work of those heroic days must not be forgotten, for they were the Port's finest hour.

## LONDON RIVER
### YESTERDAY, TO-DAY AND TO-MORROW

IN this book we have traced the story of the Port from the very beginning. We have seen how it has triumphed over every obstacle which has risen up in its path. Neither disease nor the invader, neither the irresponsibilities of its populace nor the aerial bombardment of two wars, have proved more than a temporary setback to the Port. Father Thames has always offered such advantages over other ports that his nurturing of the "hill by the pool" to the proud position of the greatest port in the world seems an almost inevitable development. Yet to-day Father Thames might well bemoan his present status and be concerned for the future. For in achieving greatness he has lost something which in earlier days was precious to him, namely, the recognition and respect of the people he has served so well; in its place he has gained the indifference of an ungrateful country. For apart from those whose livelihood is won upon the river, and others who are lucky enough to live beside its grey waters, the Thames is known to comparatively few Londoners. But this is not really the fault of the ordinary citizen, for he is not encouraged to interest himself in the river or to make use of its reaches for exercise and relaxation. The hurried though interested glances of the continuous stream of workers crossing by tram, train and motor-car are the extent of the association of the average Londoner with Father Thames. But when on 8th June 1946 he bore his Sovereign down to Westminster, with the cheers of the crowds echoing in his ears, he no doubt remembered rather wistfully the more colourful years of his life.

The esteem in which it was once held is seen by the frequent references to the "said noble river" in many old books. As London prospered it began

SPARKES YARD, LIMEHOUSE
Water colour by Dorothy Belasco

to play an increasing part in the life of the ordinary citizen, soon becoming the main thoroughfare of the City and the sporting ground for rich and poor. All day the stream was crowded with craft ferrying passengers from one part of the city to another. Between London Bridge and Chelsea there were forty-four landing-places where the general public were able to land and watermen plied their trade.

Every month this great "street" was the stage for water pageants, colourful processions and carnivals which transformed the river into a blaze of colour. The coronation processions were the most spectacular—the Royal Barge, pulled by scarlet-liveried bargemen, moved slowly up the river escorted by guard boats filled with soldiers, on whose armour and weapons the sun shone and sparkled. Following astern came the whole Court, each nobleman with his lady dressed in the glorious costume of the day. At Billingsgate the Mayor and Corporation joined the squadron in their own magnificent barges, and heralding the approach of the new King were musicians riding ahead in other craft. From many miles inland hundreds came to watch and cheer, and many hired skiffs in which they followed the fleet up to Westminster.

The hey-day of river life was the seventeenth century. "By water to Greenwich, by water to Whitehall," writes Pepys, one of the greatest

35

champions of the Thames, in his amazing diary. Court life at that time was centred in the Palace of Westminster and the Royal Barge could often be seen gliding down to Greenwich on the ebb, the rich trappings and gold scroll-work contrasting with the rough luggers of the Pool. One of the most popular entertainments was the *tableaux* which were staged in front of the Palace. Dragons and weird monsters mounted on barges and breathing forth fire and smoke were paddled past the excited crowds which had come to watch; sea-battles were fought out in miniature, and British merchantmen were raked by cannon from the Surrey shore, until the Royal Navy arrived and destroyed the enemy batteries. These pageants were followed in the evening by firework displays of extravagant proportions. On such nights the Palaces of Westminster and Lambeth were illuminated by rockets and Catherine-wheels, and trembled at the firing of blank charges.

In Pepys's day it was the custom for a new ambassador to make his first entry into London by water. Having landed at Dover he travelled by coach to Gravesend where he was met by the Lord Mayor and the City Companies. When all the formal greetings were over and the flood tide had set in, everyone embarked in barges and came the whole way up to London by water. It is a fascinating trip to-day, but in those days before the riveter's hammer was heard or the blast furnace smoked along the river banks, it must have been one of singular beauty. Kent was still a garden and the Thames a river bordered by apple orchards, meadows, and woods. As the flotilla of barges approached the City, the extent of her trade and maritime greatness caused even the shrewdest diplomat to show his admiration. At Woolwich the growing might of the Royal Navy could be seen rising on the stocks; at the bottom of Blackwall Reach the silver dome of Greenwich Palace rose from among the woods which once formed the favourite hunting-grounds of English kings. At every stroke of the oar the trots of ships grew denser, till finally, as the spires of the City churches rose above the masts in the Pool, the procession came to the Tower where everyone disembarked.

As late as 1750 the amenities offered by the Thames were exploited to the full. A favourite jaunt of Pepys's was to go by boat in the early evening up to one of the many gardens which bordered the river. Here he and his wife dined, finally returning by moonlight, the river sparkling with the fairy lights of other boats bound for the City. Yacht racing was a popular sport and much enjoyed by Charles II, who was often to be seen, periwig awry, steering his own vessel through the Pool. Rowing was the recreation of most Londoners and its popularity was still further increased by the inauguration of the race for Doggett's coat and badge in 1716. Doggett, who was something of a philanthropist and a great advocate of the Thames, was by profession a music-hall comedian. When he died he left a sum of money for the purchasing each year of an orange-coloured coat, emblazoned with the crest of the House of Hanover, which was to be presented to the

winner of a rowing race. The course was from Old Swan Stairs near London Bridge to the Old Swan Inn at Chelsea, a distance of five miles. The "coat and badge" soon became a coveted prize, and an incentive to all watermen to become more proficient. The rules specified that none could enter for the race unless he was a Freeman of the Watermen's Company, and that only six contestants could race at any one time. These rules still apply and the race, which was suspended during the war, was resumed in 1947.

As the years wore on, the star of pageantry, which had previously shone so brightly upon London's river, began to wane. The circumstances in which it had served as the main street of the capital were superseded for ever. Roads and streets began to be more than mere muddy tracks, and were made safe from the highwayman; as a result the horsedrawn carriages became fashionable, and many Thames watermen found that their services were no longer needed. Another blow was struck at the Thames when the Court, ruled by William of Orange's dislike for the river, deserted Westminster for the Palace of Kensington, where it sat desultorily till George I succeeded to the throne. For a short time river life recovered under his Royal patronage, the most famous occasion being the evening procession from Whitehall to Chelsea which must have been a most magnificent and romantic spectacle. Attended by the whole Court and accompanied by hundreds of other boats, the Royal Barge was rowed slowly up-river to the

37

sound of Handel's *Water Music*. This was played by an orchestra of fifty seated in one of the City barges, and delighted the King so much that he ordered it to be played three times in all. Since then there have been only a few occasions when the river has been allowed to play a proud part in the life of London; the funeral procession of Nelson, the opening of the new Palace of Westminster in 1847 by Queen Victoria, and of the Tower Bridge in 1894, are the most notable revivals of that splendid age, which the development of the exclusively material resources of the Port has forced into the background.

That the length of the river is no longer dotted with the craft of water-men plying their trade is understandable, for bridges, replanning, and the internal combustion engine have stolen their trade; in addition the constant dredging and canalising of the river by the various embankments have gradually changed the slow peaceful flow of the river into the three-knot tide which surges under the bridges to-day. Under such conditions it is only natural that ferrymen in their dinghies and royal processions have ceased to be a common sight on the river. That the use of the river for pleasure should take second place to the maintenance of successful commercial intercourse within the Port, is financially sound; but that interest in the river should be stifled, and that the possibilities offered by such an open space for recreation and entertainment should be neglected, is a shameful state of affairs which seems incompatible with our history.

To-day the "street" is empty, and to use Pepys's words, "there are no boats on the river." Below London Bridge there are ships of all sizes; while from the upper reaches tugs, with their lighters loaded with cargoes destined for distant lands, come bustling down to the docks; but of pleasure craft there is only a bare minimum. The reason for this is that the opportunities given for providing amenities to the public, in the form of municipal rowing and swimming clubs and, most important of all, a full-scale river excursion service, are not exploited to the full. Of rowing and sailing clubs there are a small number based between Putney and Hammer-smith. All of these entail private membership or have been organised by large businesses for the benefit of their employees. In these reaches there are other boats of many shapes and sizes, all of which are the scene of great activity at week-ends. Many of them, it is true, seldom leave their moor-ings, but show by the hours of attention which are devoted to them the love which some Londoners have for "messing about in boats." But the large majority of the public are not so fortunate, for they neither own a boat nor are able to hire one for an afternoon. Any contention that the public do not want to go out on the Thames is immediately disproved by the popularity of the existing pleasure-steamer services which, despite the handicaps of English weather, limited capital, and the poverty of piers, do a good business in the summer months. When one of these passes, it is significant to see with what interest the passengers regard everything about

THE THAMES AT CHISWICK
Oil painting by Carel Weight, 1939

them, and the rapt attention with which they listen to the eloquence of the guide; and does this interest not turn to envy when a sailing-boat, crewed by men or women, boys or girls, foams through their wake? Children on the embankment yell "give us a ride, mate"; couples cease their courting and gaze wistfully at the river, while father, out for a Sunday stroll with the family, stops and criticises the skill of the sailors. Many of them wish that they too could go out on the river and enjoy themselves in a boat for an hour or two, independent of the crowded steamer.

However, despite the efforts of various sections of the public over past years, this very natural desire remains unsatisfied. Although to all intents and purposes the interests of the Londoner on the river are still protected as in the past, the sport which his forebears enjoyed so freely seems no longer to be his established right, but rather a privilege to be exercised as little as possible. It is not my purpose here to speculate the wherefore and the why, but to consider instead any plans whereby river life can be rejuvenated, and the welfare of the citizen improved. It is only possible in this little book to dwell briefly on two such schemes; neither of these is the clamouring of ignorant visionaries, but each is the result of much hard work by a large number of eminent and practical citizens over a number of years.

The first advocates the organising of a full-scale river passenger service for pleasure purposes, and as an alternative method of transport for Londoners. In 1924 Sir Samuel Instone, after much research and trouble, forwarded a plan for a river service of twenty-five twin-screw motor vessels which were to run from Hammersmith to Woolwich. Although Sir Samuel's company were prepared to venture a considerable amount of private capital on the scheme, and were supported wholeheartedly by the Press, they were unsuccessful in convincing the London County Council of its possibilities.

In 1929 the term "Waterbus" was coined and Sir Samuel once more showed his willingness to promote a service. The London County Council once more refused to sponsor this enterprise, and rejected it on the grounds that it could only be run at a loss. However, the work still went on and in 1932 the first specifications of a waterbus to meet every condition were published. The primary function of a waterbus would be to enable those who live near the river to travel to and from work in far less tiring, and under much pleasanter, conditions than at present. It would in addition automatically alleviate traffic congestion in the City, and reduce the enforced strap-hanging, which at present makes the journey home from work so wearisome. In 1934 the waterbus was once more knocked on the head by the findings of the inquiry, which, after much representation in high places, was obtained in that year. Again it was a question of cost; the London Passenger Transport Board maintained that owing to the tidal question the regular running of a service would be uneconomic. We have already seen how the tides have influenced river life, and the paragraphs which follow should show doubly well the justification for removing this controlling force.

Within the last few years there have been a number of committees set up to inquire into the replanning of London from a social and æsthetic point of view. Many of the conclusions which have been reached have been made public through the Press, and through exhibitions at the Royal Academy, the National Gallery, and County Hall. But whatever the particular approach of these committees, each one agreed that the Thames had been shamefully neglected during the last few years, and provided great scope for broad and imaginative planning in the future. If the plans suggested by the Royal Academy, and depicted by J. D. M. Harvey in *London Replanned*, are realised, the vistas which will be opened up for river-goers will be magnificent.

The second scheme recommends a tideless Thames through the construction of a "barrage." We cannot deal with this in detail proportionate to the revolutionary effect which its adoption would have on the whole Port.

PENANG GRAIN SHIP AT MILLWALL SILO

Water colour by Norman James, 1935

CHISWICK REACH AT LOW TIDE SEEN FROM AN UPPER WINDOW IN HAMMERSMITH TERRACE

Oil painting by Gwen Herbert, 1943

To-day the idea that the greater part of the Thames should be made tide-less astonishes the ordinary citizen and alarms the local authority. This is largely due to ignorance of what the present situation is within the Port, and of the consequences which the construction of a barrage across the Thames would have on the upper reaches. The commercial and social advantages which London would enjoy as a result of such action appear so conclusive that it is difficult to see why this proposal has not already been inquired into by the relevant authority.

The plan to build a barrage across the Thames was initiated as early as 1858. Since then the subject has been raised three or four times, but each attempt to invoke an official investigation has proved unsuccessful. How-ever, not one of these has been entirely fruitless, for to-day the project is backed by a vast amount of data, the result of many years of study and research. First the plan failed because the London sewerage problem had not been solved by the present Barking-Crossness system of discharges. Next in 1881 it was argued that a dam would silt up the river. In 1902 Mr. Thomas W. Barber, M.Inst.C.E., planned the construction of a barrage at Gravesend. This proposal was defeated by the findings of the Royal Commission which had been set up to inquire into the state of the Port, whose fortunes, it will be remembered, had at that time sunk to a low ebb. The committee, in view of the circumstances, did not look favourably on any plan which was not relevant to and likely to remedy the immediate problem, and consequently rejected the Gravesend barrage. In 1921 the manager of a large steamship company advocated the policy of a tideless Thames at an engineering congress held in London; the only effect of this brave-hearted appeal was to arouse the wrath and odium of his fellow congress-members.

Finally, in 1935, the Thames Barrage Association was founded. This Association, whose fine and altruistic work is comparatively unknown in England, let alone acknowledged, produced two schemes for the construc-tion of a barrage across the Thames; the first in 1935 and the second in 1938. The subject of both was the construction of a barrage at the junction of Woolwich and Gallions Reaches. The second project was a modification of the first and an answer to the fears held by the Committee of Imperial Defence and the P.L.A. on the disastrous consequences following a success-ful aerial bombardment on such a barrage. It was on these grounds that the inquiry, forced on the Port of London Authority in 1938, was vetoed twenty-four hours before it was due to start sitting.

The essentials of both plans are similar but they differ in detail. Each plan embodies locks, sluices and a roadway in the one unit. But whereas the 1935 scheme consists simply of seven locks, three large and four smaller ones situated in the centre of the dam, the locking arrangements in the later plan are dispersed over a mile. In the latter scheme, ships of comparatively small size would pass through the locks situated at each end of the barrage.

while large ships would use those at the entrance to the 500-ft. ship canal. This plan possesses many advantages over its earlier brother, and is the one most likely to be forwarded by the Thames Barrage Association in the future. However, we need not concern ourselves here so much with the details of the barrage as with the general pros and cons of the enterprise, and the reasons which prompt the Association to continue their work.

The construction of the barrage proposed by the Association would result in the river above Woolwich becoming tideless. The rate of flow would be controlled by the head of water passing over Teddington weir, and by the sluice gates of the barrage itself. Those in opposition maintain that this would cause the Thames to become a stagnant lake, but the Association, basing their beliefs on extensive scientific research, reply that far from making the river dirtier, their scheme could not help but make the river considerably cleaner than at present. From the Barking-Crossness outlets, over 270 million gallons of sewage are discharged into the river daily. The volume of this is so great that the water in Gallions Reach is incapable of acting as an efficient diluent, with the result that unoxidised sewage is borne up to London on the flood tide. This deplorable situation would certainly be remedied by a barrage as the proposed site is above the main discharges. However, the most beneficial effect would be the continuous access to every dock and wharf above Woolwich. Instead of ships having to time their arrival in the Pool or at the entrance to one of the docks according to the tide, the constant high-water level would enable ships to lock in and out whenever they liked. At present the handling of goods and the loading and unloading of ships is governed in no small way by the tide and the imperative need for "catching" it when it is high. Owing to unforeseen circumstances, it is not always possible to do this and the result is overtime pay, demurrage, and a needless increase in the expenses of merchants and shipowners. It is significant, therefore, that London is to-day one of the most expensive ports in the world.

The Association next draw attention to the increased facilities which a barrage would give to Londoners for sport and recreation generally. Handicapped no more by stretches of oozing and evil-smelling mud, rowing and sailing clubs could be organised in many other reaches instead of only in two or three; there the placid lake, polluted no more by multifarious flotsam and jetsam, would offer splendid opportunities for bathing and water sports in general. Even for those of us who have lived near the river all our lives and have become inured to the colour of the water, the flow of filth which nowadays permeates the uppermost reaches makes swimming in the Thames a pleasure of the past. There is no denying the fact that the river gets dirtier every year. A few years ago boys and girls spent many pleasant hours fishing for dace and sticklebacks, and no doubt they would do so still if it was not that every form of fish has long since been driven far up the river, or poisoned by the impurities in the water.

THE THAMES BARRAGE AS IT MIGHT BE
Water colour by A. van Anrooy, 1935

These three points alone seem to provide a strong enough case for recognition of the Association's plan, and till we inquire further, we can only presume that the steadfast opposition with which it has always been met is due to an equally imposing number of disadvantages.

First on the list is the traditional contention that the river would become an almost stagnant stream. The fallacy of this argument is that the decomposition of waste matter in water depends more on the quantity of oxygen in the water than the speed at which the river is flowing.

Secondly, the "Noes" believe that the locking capacity afforded by the barrage would be insufficient for the trade of the Port, resulting in ships having to queue up before passing the dam. The accuracy of this statement is obviously of overwhelming importance. However, the Thames Barrage Association, having collected the figures of shipping movements in the Port during one calendar month, maintain that not only does their proposal leave a wide margin for any sudden increase in traffic but also allows for the number of locks to be increased if necessary.

One indisputable result of a barrage is the need which would automatically arise for a new system of supplying the power companies of London with coal. Under the present method they run their own private fleet of colliers. These ships, because they have to make fast coastwise passages in all sorts of weather, are large in tonnage, and have a high bridge superstructure on the stern. Their ungainly appearance in the narrow upper reaches has earned them the derogatory name of "flatirons." When any of these are bound for wharves above the Pool, they have to race the tide in order to reach their destination on time and to avoid being trapped

43

between reaches with insufficient head-room underneath the bridges farther up-river. If there was a constant high-water level above Woolwich, the flatirons would be unable to reach, among others, the power stations at Battersea and Fulham. Neither the lowering of the upperworks of the colliers nor the raising of the combings of the river bridges form practicable solutions to the problem. To counter this difficulty the Thames Barrage Association have proposed that a special berth be built near the barrage, where the flatirons could transfer their cargoes into large barges such as those used on the Rhine. Although this would eliminate the problem of head-room, the power companies are prejudiced against it on the grounds that the double handling of coal would cause added delays and additional costs.

This disagreement constitutes the greatest embarrassment to the barrage scheme, but it is surely not one of such intricacy that it cannot be settled by mutual co-operation. Having raised the sympathy of over twenty-one riverside boroughs, many important committees, and a number of Members of Parliament during recent years, the Association hope that their assiduous efforts will at least merit a full public inquiry.

## CONCLUSION

B EFORE we end, we must dwell on certain features of our story which though they may be of little material value, should be of wide interest to the ordinary citizen.

The beauty and charm of the Port of London is seldom acknowledged, for her riparian architecture is not on the grandiose lines of that of Paris, Budapest, and other capital cities: London's commercial greatness, and the unimaginative planning of her civil authorities through the centuries, is responsible for the present shabby appearance of certain parts of the water-front. But few rivers possess such character and offer such a variety of æsthetic attractions as the Thames. Its many reaches form an ever-changing panorama which can only be properly appreciated from the deck of a small boat. When chugging up the river from Southend, the mariner cannot but marvel at the kaleidoscopic quality of the river. As he passes from one reach to the next, the scene may shift from one of commercial magnificence to one of rural simplicity; regal palaces stand incongruously beside smoking factories, quaint riverside houses break the line of busy docks, children, in summer months, paddle on the sandy beach below the Tower of London; in this way the face of the river-front changes, each new vista being coloured by countless associations past and present.

Although unknown to many Londoners, the river has never failed to attract a large number of artists to its banks. Hogarth and Canaletto, Turner and Whistler are perhaps the most famous of their number.

44

ON THE TIDE TO LONDON
Oil painting by Arthur J. W. Burgess, 1945

Although each one applied his art differently, all recognised the paintable qualities of the river, whether it was the tranquillity of the upper reaches, or the picturesqueness of the Pool, with its crowded shipping and bay-windowed taverns. Of all the great artists of the past, Turner had a special love of the Thames, beside which he spent the greater part of his life. Having lived first at Hammersmith, then at Twickenham, he moved in his last years to a house on Cheyne Walk. It was when living here, in 1839, that he painted his magnificent picture of "The Fighting *Téméraire*" being towed to the ship-breaker's yard at Rotherhithe.

The Thames in those days must have been a magnificent sight for, till the middle of the century, ship-building was still the predominant industry in the Port. From the days of Alfred the Great, ships have sailed down the Thames on their maiden voyages, and won wealth and renown for England: the *Henri Grace à Dieu*, built at Erith in 1512 by Henry VIII, the *Sovereign of the Seas*, at Woolwich, the dignified frigates from the Blackwall Yard, and lastly H.M.S. *Thunderer*, a dreadnought of 23,000 tons, mounting four 13·5 inch guns, and launched as recently as 1910, are a few examples of Thames ship-building through the ages.

The first successful transatlantic crossings under steam, by the *Sirius* and *Great Western* in 1838, heralded the passing of sail. Not even the failure of the *Great Eastern*, launched from a Millwall yard in 1858, could alter what destiny had obviously decreed. The development of screw-propulsion, and the opening of the Suez Canal in 1869, assured the world of the eventual supremacy of steam. With every year the size of ships increased, till gradually London ship-builders realised that conditions had turned against them; they therefore devoted all their efforts and enterprise to ship-repairing, in which capacity they were so successful that London has for many years now been the greatest ship-repairing port in the kingdom. In spite of our steadily expanding fleet of merchant ships a vestige of the old days still remained. Clippers brought tea from China, and wind-jammers continued for many years to berth in the Millwall Dock, after sailing in the great Grain Race from Australia. With the turn of the century these wonderful ships began to fade from the Thames picture, till now the only reminder of the days of sail rests in the hard-working Sprit-sail Barge. It is feared by many that these too are doomed by the ever-quickening step of commerce, but while they live they remain the most lovely ships on London River; it is grand to see them punching their way up-river, with their heavy red-ochre sails full-bellied with wind, being handled as easily as a pram-dinghy by the diminutive figure on the stern. These barges are generally registered at Rochester, but carry their 100–300-ton cargoes of bricks, cement and timber between East Coast ports and the Thames. A few miles above Tilbury, in St. Clement's Reach, lies the fairest clipper ever built, the *Cutty Sark*. Now in company with an old-time ship of the line, the *Worcester*, she is ending her days as a boys' training ship.

At the top of the next reach, Long Reach, there is an attractive village called Purfleet. Legend relates that its name is derived from Queen Elizabeth's bitter comment, "Oh, my poor fleet," after she had reviewed some of her ships here before they set out to meet the Spanish Armada. As he turns into Greenwich Reach, the sailor obtains one of the finest views of London. The magnificent proportions of what is now the Royal Naval College are seen in contrast to the excessively drab appearance of the Isle of Dogs opposite. This curious title for what is now a busy industrial area is attributed to the Royal kennels which were built there when Greenwich Park was one of the royal hunting-grounds.

Ports and public-houses are co-existent all the world over, but those on Thames-side have a quality of their own. Dwarfed between towering warehouses and overhanging the river, each one boasts a brightly painted sign which welcomes the waterman as he comes ashore in his little rowing-boat. At the top of Limehouse Reach leans "The Grapes," said to be characterised by Dickens in *Our Mutual Friend* as the "Six Jolly Fellowship Porters." This is a particularly attractive corner of the river, for there are often a number of Thames barges and other boats moored beneath its tiny

THE BRICKLAYER'S ARMS, LIMEHOUSE
Water colour by an unknown artist, 1790

saloon window. Entering the Lower Pool we pass the much-favoured "Prospect of Whitby" which, in good times, always looks very smart with its white-and-black timbers, its green sign, and flowering geraniums. Beside Wapping Old Stairs is "The Town of Ramsgate," noteworthy only as being the place where Judge Jeffreys was arrested. The interior of many of these taverns is often disappointingly lacking in romance, for much of their attraction lies in their names and their association with the river.

Tower Bridge is always a welcome sight to the sailor, for it symbolises his safe landfall. Having passed beneath its great bascules we enter the Upper Pool, and see first the Tower, and then Billingsgate Market, the fishing port of London. After shooting Southwark Bridge we catch a momentary but unforgettable glimpse of St. Paul's rising behind the old "port" of Queenhythe, its silver dome ethereal above the sordid ugliness of the warehouses.

And so the Port stretches westwards, revealing all the time new delights and different aspects of its character: County Hall, leading to the Houses of Parliament; at the top of Royal Reach, the simple but impressive mass of Battersea power station, followed by the delicacy of Cheyne Walk at Chelsea; Hammersmith, "The Doves," Chiswick Eyot and The Mall, Kew and Strand-on-the-Green.

47

As the river narrows, trade gives way to the picturesque, till at Brentford it dies altogether, and willow trees succeed the hard-working crane. As an example of the loveliness of certain reaches of the Thames, Syon Reach, above Brentford, is outstanding.

Here the heron, paddling in the shallows with neck outstretched, makes his lightning jabs at the water, till he rises, warned by his uncanny instinct of the approach of a human, and flaps his way slowly inland. In summer months ducks paddle noisily in and out of the rushes, pursued feverishly by their fluffy families, delighting the pedestrian on the leafy towing-path, the mariner in his boat, and the tripper in the pleasure steamer. Here then, the Thames throws off his mantle of commerce and dons a cloak of green. At the top of the reach lies Isleworth, with its Georgian houses and classic inn, "The London Apprentice," while three miles farther on we come to Teddington, the landward limit of the Port.

After even this brief excursion surely few can deny that the Port of London is a fascinating and wonderful waterway? Its importance to Britain can never be over-stressed, especially to-day when it is imperative that our commerce be expedited by every possible means. London is the largest manufacturing city in Great Britain, and before the war her docks handled a third of the country's total exports and imports. But in addition to satisfying her own wants, London's *entrepôt* trade is the greatest in the world, and of supreme financial benefit to England. Immense quantities of goods are shipped into the Thames, not for our own consumption, but for storage, sale, and eventual distribution to other countries. This incoming wealth of goods has in the past made the Port of London the market and financial centre of the world. Let us hope that in future these high-sounding titles will be equally true, for as long as the heart beats strongly in the "hill by the pool," the fortunes of England will be assured.

## SHORT BIBLIOGRAPHY

*London's Natural History* by R. S. R. Fitter. 1945, Collins.—*History of the Port of London* by Sir Joseph Broodbank. 2 vols. 1921, O'Connor. —*Port of London Authority 1909–1934* by Alan Bell. 1934, P.L.A.—*Lure and Lore of London's River* by A. G. Linney. 1932, Sampson Low.— *No Boats on the River* by A. P. Herbert. 1932, Methuen.—*Tideless Thames in Future London* by J. H. O. Bunge. 1944, Muller